Beautiful Butterflies o

A Nature on Our Doorstep Book

Comma and Peacock on blackthorn

Annette Meredith

with photographs by Ian Lindsay and Annette Meredith

For my grandchildren

With thanks to my children for their assistance and encouragement
and to Ted for his ever-patient support and advice.

Many thanks to Ian Lindsay for providing me with so many beautiful photos: Brimstone, Brown Argus, Common Blue,
Gatekeeper, Green Hairstreak, Green-veined White, Large White, Large Skipper, Meadow Brown, Peacock, Ringlet,
Silver-studded Blue, Silver-washed Fritillary, Swallowtail, Small Skipper, Speckled Wood and White-letter Hairstreak butterflies;
Marsh Fritillary larva, pupa and imago; Orange-tip egg, larva, pupa and imago; Painted Lady larva;
Cinnabar moth and larva; Garden Tiger moth and larva;
Brimstone, Emperor, Mint and Six-spot Burnet moths, and Pale Tussock cocoon.

Grateful thanks to Peter Eeles of ukbutterflies.co.uk for so generously contributing the photos
of a Marsh Fritillary laying eggs (p.12), Large Blue butterfly (p.7), and Small Tortoiseshell pupa (p13).

Thanks also to Joe Schelling for the photos of Small Blue, Dingy Skipper, Dark Green Fritillary,
Small White, and Large White on dandelion.

Thanks to Ben Smith for the photo of the Meadow Brown butterfly in grass and Spindle Ermine Moth webs.

Cover photo of Red Admiral on sedum by Annette Meredith.
Photo on cover page of Comma and Peacock butterflies by Annette Meredith, taken in Jubilee Country Park, London.

Butterflies (and Moths) you'll find in this book

	Page
Brimstone *(Gonepteryx rhamni)*	19
Brown Argus *(Aricia agestis)*	36
Brown Hairstreak *(Thecla betulae)*	36
Clouded Yellow *(Colias croceus)*	23
Comma *(Polygonia c-album)*	30
Common Blue *(Polyommatus icarus)*	5, 25
Dark Green Fritillary *(Argynnis aglaja)*	34
Dingy Skipper *(Erynnis tages)*	33
Gatekeeper *(Pyronia tithonus)*	30
Green Hairstreak *(Callophrys rubi)*	34
Green-veined White *(Pieris napi)*	36
Heath Fritillary *(Melitaea Athalia)*	35
Holly Blue *(Celastrina argiolus)*	36
Large Blue *(Phengaris arion)*	7
Large Tortoiseshell *(Nymphalis polychloros)*	8
Large Skipper *(Ochlodes Sylvanus)*	33
Large White *(Pieris brassicae)*	11, 17, 20, 37
Marsh Fritillary *(Euphydryas aurinia)*	12
Meadow Brown *(Maniola jurtina)*	30, 39
Monarch *(Danaus Plexippus)*	14, 15
Orange-Tip *(Anthocharis cardamines)*	10, 11
Painted Lady *(Vanessa cardui)*	4, 21, 22
Peacock *(Inachis io)*	4, 18, 29
Red Admiral *(Vanessa atalanta)*	23, 24, 38
Ringlet *(Aphantopus hyperantus)*	36
Silver-studded Blue *(Plebeius argus)*	36
Silver-washed Fritillary *(Argynnis paphia)*	9
Small Blue *(Cupido minimus)*	6
Small Copper *(Lycaena phlaeas)*	28
Small Skipper *(Thymelicius silvestris)*	32
Small Tortoiseshell *(Aglais urticae)*	8, 13
Small White *(Pieris rapae)*	37
Speckled Wood *(Pararge aegeria)*	28
Swallowtail *(Papilio machaon)*	27
Wall *(Lasiommata megera)*	30
White-letter Hairstreak *(Satyrium w-album)*	34

Moths

Brimstone *(Opisthograptis luteolata)*

	Page
Cinnabar *(Tyria jacobaeae)*	26
Emperor *(Saturnia pavonia)*	25
Garden Tiger *(Arctia caja)*	26
Hummingbird Hawk-moth	26
(Macroglossum stellatarum)	
Mint *(Pyrausta aurata)*	26
Pale Tussock *(Calliteara pudibunda)*	26
Six-spot Burnet	26
(Zygaena filipendulae)	
Spindle Ermine	31
(Yponomeuta cagnagella)	

Silver-washed Fritillary and Jersey Tiger Moth on Hemp Agrimony

Part One – Not Just a Pretty Face

Ask your grandparents if they remember seeing a lot more butterflies in their gardens when they were young than they do today, and they will probably say "yes".

Painted Lady

wingspan: 50 – 56 mm

Preferred Host Plant: thistles

Painted Lady and Peacock butterflies on Butterfly Bush

Peacock

wingspan: 63 – 69 mm

Host Plant: common nettle

Habitat – the natural environment that has everything a creature needs for its survival.

Why are there fewer butterflies now than there were fifty years ago? There are many reasons, but one of the main ones is loss of habitat. When houses and factories and roads are built, and when fields and gardens are sprayed with pesticides, the natural habitat of many creatures, including butterflies, is lost.

Scientists have been studying butterflies for a long time. Because butterflies are such an important part of the ecosystem and they are easily affected by any changes in the weather or their habitat, they can tell us a lot about what is happening to the environment.

When we see a lot of butterflies and moths, we know that we have a healthy ecosystem. That means there will also be plenty of other insects and many different plants for them all to feed on.

Common Blue

Plants are important for lots of reasons. They not only provide food for insects and many other creatures (including us), they also clean the air that we breathe. Intensive farming has often meant that we have lost ancient woodland, heath land and flower-rich meadows. Also, the routine spraying of crops with insecticides and herbicides affects the entire food chain, not just insects.

Herbicide – a chemical used to kill specific plants.

Ecosystem – A community of living and non-living things (water, soil, air, plants and everything living) that work together to create a balance.

Different butterflies have particular plants that they like, called host plants. There may be several host plants in the same family, but some butterflies only lay eggs on one distinct species. When wildlife habitat is fragmented (for example when a housing estate is built on land that was once a meadow or woodland, or when land is planted with a single species of non-native trees), the habitat that is left is much smaller. More creatures compete for the resources and sometimes a particular food source is lost altogether in that area. If that food source is the only host plant for a specific butterfly, it can drive that species to extinction in that particular location.

wingspan: 20 – 30 mm

Small Blue

male

Kidney vetch is the only host plant for the Small Blue.

The Small Blue is Britain's smallest butterfly. There are nine resident species of little blue butterflies, although they are not always blue. Small Blue males' upperwings are very dark and the female is a dusky brown colour. The Large Blue disappeared from the UK over forty years ago, but has since been successfully re-introduced.

Large Blue

wingspan:
38 – 44 mm

Host Plant: wild thyme

Bringing back the Large Blue to the British countryside took years of work, but now the population is estimated to be more than 10,000. In order to bring back a species to an area, you cannot just bring in butterflies from other places and hope they'll thrive. The Large Blue needs a particular type of grassland habitat and that had to be re-created first. Not only did there need to be wild thyme (the Large Blue's host plant) but there also needed to be colonies of a specific species of red ant. That's because the Large Blue has an unusual life cycle – the caterpillars initially feed on wild thyme, but later fall to the ground and trick the red ants into thinking that they are one of their own. Once in the ant colony, they become carnivorous and feed on ant grubs through the winter until pupating and emerging as a butterfly in spring.

There are around 180,000 species of Lepidoptera around the world. Of these, only a tiny fraction – perhaps 200 – are carnivorous.

Lepidoptera – an order of insects that includes butterflies and moths.

Sometimes a species reappears and no one is quite sure why. Until the early 1960s the Large Tortoiseshell was a common butterfly in the UK, but several factors caused its numbers to decline and for many years it has been considered extinct here. One major reason is that its preferred host plant is the elm tree and Dutch Elm disease has killed millions of trees in Britain over the past few decades, with not many elms surviving.

wingspan: 68 – 75 mm

Large Tortoiseshell

Recently, conservationists have discovered that this beautiful butterfly is breeding in a small area of Dorset and there is now optimism that the Large Tortoiseshell may start to once again be seen in the countryside and in our gardens.

Conservationists, scientists and nature lovers all play a vital role in helping butterlies to survive and thrive. Understanding the needs and life cycles of different butterflies helps us to make sure that they will still be here for future generations to enjoy.

Apart from size, the main difference between these two butterflies is that the Small Tortoiseshell has a greater area of black on the hindwings and is generally more colourful.

Small Tortoiseshell

Host Plant: common nettle

wingspan: 50 – 56 mm

Part Two – The Amazing Metamorphosis

Butterflies are part of the insect kingdom. An insect has six legs and an exoskeleton, which means its supporting skeleton is on the outside of its body. It's a bit like wearing a suit of armor!

Insects also have three body parts (head, thorax and abdomen), two antennae, and compound eyes.

forewing

veins

compound eye

antenna

hindwing

proboscis

abdomen

thorax

Silver-washed Fritillary

wingspan: 72 – 76 mm

Host Plant: common dog-violet

All butterflies go through four stages – egg (ovum), caterpillar (larva), pupa (chrysalis) and butterfly (imago). Butterflies may live for a few days or as long as a year, depending not just on the species but also on the time of year that their eggs hatch.

The female butterfly lays eggs on the host plant, often on the underside of a leaf. The eggs don't fall off because she attaches them with special glue that she makes.

Egg laid by an Orange-tip

Orange-tip caterpillar

Orange-tip pupa

girdle

Some butterflies prefer to lay one egg per plant to make sure that the new caterpillar will have plenty of food to eat.

Some caterpillars make a silk "girdle" to attach the chrysalis to a stem or twig.

Some butterflies lay eggs underneath a leaf and some lay them on top. Eggs are always laid on host plants so that the caterpillars have the right food to eat. Once they become butterflies, they can drink nectar from many different flowers.

Orange-tip butterfly

male

wingspan:
45 - 50 mm

female

underwing

Favourite Host Plants:
cuckooflower and garlic mustard

Although many butterfly names give a clue as to what they might look like – here it is obvious how the orange-tip got its name – it is also quite easy to mistake one species of butterfly for another.

Large White

Wingspan:
63 - 70mm

Favourite Host Plants:
cabbage and brussel sprouts

At first glance, you might look at this butterfly and decide that this is also a female Orange-tip, but look again, because it's not. Examine it more carefully and you'll see that this butterfly has an extra black spot on its wings. If you compare these butterflies

Large White

when both have their wings folded, you'll see how different they look. Always watch a butterfly for a while before you identify it.

Many birds like to eat caterpillars. Some birds make sure that they have their families at a time when there are lots of caterpillars around. The baby birds in the nest are always hungry and a caterpillar provides a nutritious meal. From egg to butterfly, every stage produces a tasty snack for someone in the food chain. That's why butterflies lay a lot of eggs – many of them won't get further than the caterpillar stage before they are eaten.

Marsh Fritillary laying eggs

Marsh Fritillary caterpillar

Marsh Fritillary pupa

Marsh Fritillary butterfly

Wingspan: 43 – 48mm

Main Host Plants: devil's bit scabious (1), field scabious (2)

Marsh fritillaries used to be more common in the UK but are now only found on the western side of Britain and Ireland. Britain has eight species of resident fritillaries, and several are threatened due to loss of habitat.

The first stage of the caterpillar, called the first instar, is so tiny that often it isn't noticed by predators. The caterpillars of some butterflies, like the Comma, start off looking like bird droppings.

Even though it's tiny it soon grows, because it eats…and eats. After several days of constant eating, a caterpillar gets too big for its own skin. So, what does it do? Its skin splits and falls off and a new, bigger caterpillar emerges.

Larva shedding skin

Small Tortoiseshell caterpillar

cremaster
Small Tortoiseshell ready to pupate

Small Tortoiseshells lay their eggs on stinging nettles, but when the caterpillar is ready to pupate it looks for a safe place that may be nearby, or may be some distance away.

wings
Small Tortoiseshell chrysalis

Many caterpillars hang upside down in a "J" shape before pupating. Then they spin silk and attach themselves to a stem with a hook-like appendage called a cremaster that is embedded in the silk. When they are ready to emerge you can often see their markings.

13

Metamorphosis is a word that comes from Greek and it means transformation or "the state or condition of changing shape". You would think that we have always known that caterpillars turn into butterflies, but it was not until the late 17th century that a German painter, scientist and naturalist, Maria Sybilla Merian, published books depicting the metamorphosis of moths and butterflies. In 1705, her book showing the full life cycle of tropical insects and their food plants created a sensation across Europe. She was truly a woman who was ahead of her time.

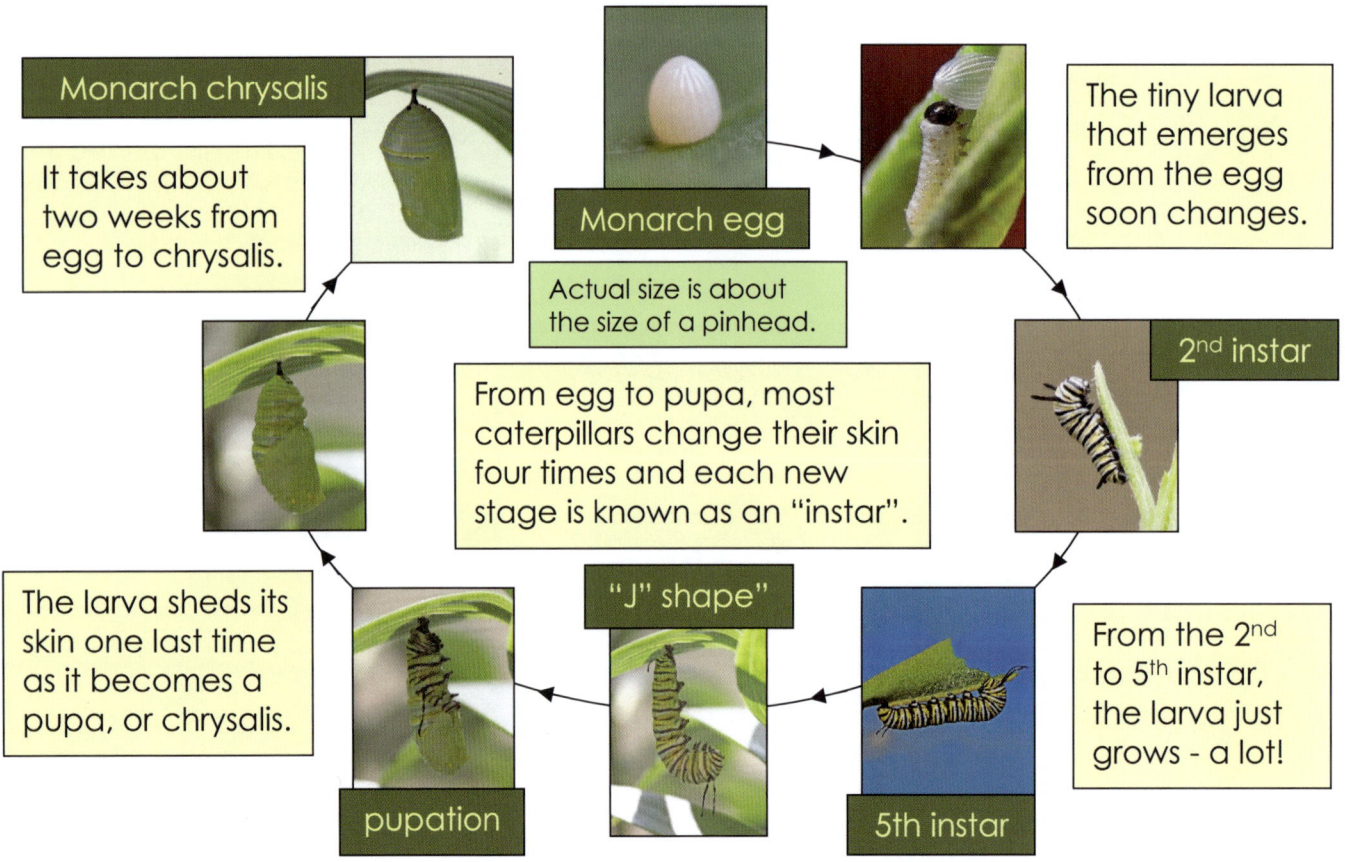

Monarch chrysalis

It takes about two weeks from egg to chrysalis.

Monarch egg

Actual size is about the size of a pinhead.

The tiny larva that emerges from the egg soon changes.

From egg to pupa, most caterpillars change their skin four times and each new stage is known as an "instar".

2nd instar

The larva sheds its skin one last time as it becomes a pupa, or chrysalis.

"J" shape"

pupation

5th instar

From the 2nd to 5th instar, the larva just grows - a lot!

14

The Monarch butterfly is one of the most studied in the world. It is an amazing butterfly, making one of the longest journeys of any butterfly on its annual migration to Mexico from as far north as Canada. It is also interesting to study because it is so dependent on milkweed, its only host plant.

Eclosion of a Monarch butterfly

Chrysalis (day 12)

The Monarch chrysalis turns from green to almost black in the day before it ecloses. Monarch butterflies are occasionally sighted in the UK, but they are not native to Europe and can only breed in places where their host plant, milkweed, grows.

Eclosion – the emergence of an adult insect from a pupa.

Female Monarch

Caterpillar frass (magnified)

With all the eating that caterpillars have to do, they poop – a lot!

Caterpillar poop is called frass and it's really good for the soil.

Nutrient – a substance that provides the energy and nourishment that animals and plants need to help them grow and survive.

In rainforests, frass plays a vitally important role in the ecosystem by recycling nutrients from the leaves that have been eaten. Even in your own garden, it can help to feed the soil so that plants will grow bigger and produce more flowers. It also helps the plants to be stronger and better able to fight against disease.

People who don't understand how an ecosystem works think that because the caterpillars are eating their plants, they need to kill them. When they do, there is a risk that the ecosystem will get out of balance. The plants can grow new leaves and in the end are usually helped rather than hurt by the caterpillars.

Eggs, caterpillars and the butterflies they change into are an important source of food for many creatures.

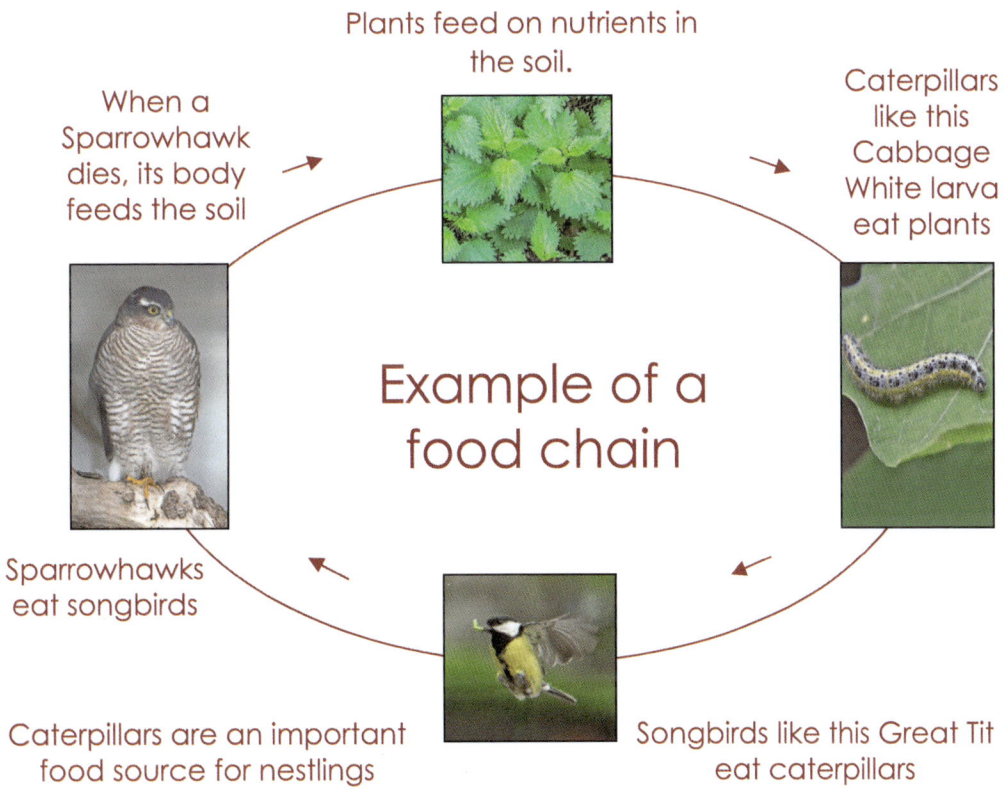

Plants feed on nutrients in the soil.

When a Sparrowhawk dies, its body feeds the soil

Caterpillars like this Cabbage White larva eat plants

Example of a food chain

Sparrowhawks eat songbirds

Caterpillars are an important food source for nestlings

Songbirds like this Great Tit eat caterpillars

In a food chain, energy is passed from one link to another. All food chains start with plants, which get their energy from the sun and the soil. Most creatures eat more than one type of food, so food chains are normally food webs with more than one link. If a link ever disappears, for example if there were no caterpillars for the birds to eat, the whole food chain would be affected.

We've looked at the four stages in the life cycle of a butterly (or moth), but how long does each stage take? Well, that depends on a lot of things, including the weather, but the main differences depend on which species of butterfly you are considering.

Let's look at the life cycle of one of our best-known butterflies, the Peacock, as an example.

Peacocks lay eggs in May and caterpillars start appearing in mid-May, as many as 500 on one plant; they take between one and three weeks to hatch. Peacock caterpillars spin a communal web and mass together, perhaps because there is safety in numbers. Later, they find a place to pupate alone.

Peacock caterpillars and chrysalis

Peacock

Peacocks are one of the few species that we may see at any time of year, but the most likely months are from March to May or July to September. Adults find dark, safe places to hibernate and you may spot one on a warm, spring morning. They can live up to 11 months, a long time for a butterfly.

There are 59 butterfy species seen regularly in the UK; two of these (the Painted Lady and Clouded Yellow) are migrants, spending winter in warmer climes. Nine of the 59 species overwinter as eggs, 31 spend the winter hibernating as caterpillars, eleven overwinter as a chrysalis, five overwinter as an adult butterfly (imago) and one (the Speckled Wood) overwinters as either a caterpillar or a chrysalis.

Adult butterflies usually only live for a few weeks, so you need to know when they are likely to be around if you're going on a butterfly hunt. Luckily for us, the most common butterfly visitors to our gardens are also often the longest-lived.

Peacocks, Red Admirals, Painted Ladies, Commas and Brimstones may be seen in any month of the year, although mostly in the summer months (not so much in June).

Brimstones roost in trees at night. Their wings look like leaves and provide good camouflage against predators. Eggs are laid in April and May; caterpillars are seen from May through July.

Female Brimstone

Wingspan: 60mm

Male

Host Plant: buckthorn

This Brimstone has just eclosed and is drying its wings. Female Brimstones are pale green or whitish.

Most caterpillars hang upside down before they pupate, although a few (like the Large White) spin a "girdle" to attach themselves to a twig, stem or other surface in an upright position. The chrysalis goes into a dormant stage, although it will wiggle and move slightly to deter predators if it's disturbed. Its outer skin hardens and it slowly turns into a pupa, also called a chrysalis. While the outside of the chrysalis hardens like a shell, inside the chrysalis a lot is happening. This stage can last from several days to several months. Caterpillars born in the autumn often remain dormant throughout the winter months.

Large White Chrysalis

Dormant – as if in a very deep sleep.

The pupa doesn't eat at all. Inside the shell the chrysalis is undergoing metamorphosis and slowly changing into a butterfly. This Large White chrysalis has been dormant all through the cold days of winter, but it's just waiting for some warm spring days.

Although they all metamorphose, each species has its own specific needs and its own characteristics.

Large White on dandelion

Part Three – Butterfly Migration

We've seen how important it is to understand the life cycle of butterflies if we want to know how to attract them to our gardens or when and where to look for a particular species.

The Monarch butterfly is the most famous for making a journey of thousands of miles to its wintering grounds in Mexico, but we have two species of butterfly in Britain that migrate and one of them, especially, makes an equally impressive journey.

Painted Lady

It was only about a decade ago that we found out how truly remarkable the Painted Lady's journey is. Researchers and scientists analysed data from thousands of sightings across Europe and this small butterfly, weighing less than one gram, was found to be travelling vast distances by riding favourable wind currents at high altitudes. Rather than being at the mercy of the wind, as previously thought, Painted Ladies fly too high to be seen on their southern migration as they head for tropical Africa.

Painted Lady caterpillar

Painted Lady on aster

Painted Ladies visit the UK for the summer months, and the last generation born in autumn is the one that makes the long journey south. Because the adults only live for two to four weeks, it will be successive generations of Painted Ladies that travel north in spring, so it will be their great-great-great grandchildren who return.

We still don't fully understand how migrating butterflies find their way across continents to places they have never been before, but it is thought that they use the sun and moon to navigate. Warming or cooling temperatures and day length are the main factors that trigger migration.

The Painted Lady is the most widespread butterfly species in the world. From April to October, it's the butterfly you're most likely to see in the UK, especially if you have a garden full of flowers.

Painted Lady caterpillars are able to feed on over 300 different host plants, and some of those are flowers like hollyhock, mallows and aster, which are common in gardens.

Painted Lady on zinnia

The Clouded Yellow is the other butterfly that migrates from north Africa and southern Europe, with numbers varying each year. As the climate warms, they are spotted in more areas of Britain, but most are seen in southern England from early July to the end of October.
They are known for years of spectacular mass migration known as "Clouded Yellow Years", and it is thought that some now overwinter in southern England.

Wingspan: 57 - 62mm

Clouded Yellow

Main Host Plants: legumes and clovers

Although Painted Ladies and Clouded Yellows are true migrants, with few or none overwintering in the UK, there are other species of butterfly and moth that may or may not migrate.

For example, Red Admirals also migrate to Europe and North Africa, although some spend winter in the southernmost parts of the UK. The Red Admiral is another butterfly that is common in many other parts of the world, including Asia and North America, migrating to warmer regions for the winter months.

Butterflies like the nectar from fruit blossoms, but some, like this Red Admiral, also enjoy juice from the fruit.

Part Four – Every Colour Under the Sun

Iridescent – shining with many different colours from different angles.

Wingspan: 67 - 72mm

Host Plant: stinging nettle

Red Admiral

For centuries, butterflies have been admired for their beauty. One of the reasons butterflies amaze us with their wonderful colours is that they have iridescent scales on their wings. Their wings are covered in hundreds of thousands of tiny scales that reflect the light. Many also have ultraviolet colours on their wings. These cannot be seen by us, but they can be seen by other butterflies. There is a secret world of colour that we don't even realise is there.

There are more than 17,500 species of butterfly in the world, but If you wanted to know more about every one of the 59 species seen regularly in the UK, you could easily learn to recognise them all. Most of these butterflies prefer grass, heath or woodland so you will need to visit a nature reserve or country park if you want to see a greater variety of butterflies.

It would be harder to learn about all the moths; there are many more species of moth than there are butterflies - over 160,000 species of moth worldwide. Around 2,500 of these species can be found in the UK.

Common Blue

Is it a butterfly or a moth?

Moth antennae are usually feathery or fringed, with no "club".

Butterfly antennae have a "club" shape at the end.

Wingspan: 35mm

Host Plant: Bird's-foot-trefoil

Wingspan: 55 - 80mm

Emperor Moth

Moths are often thought of as being dull in colour, but there are many beautiful moths. Moths tend to have furry bodies and they rest with their wings open – butterflies usually rest with their wings closed.

Although most moths are nocturnal, coming out at night, there are moths that fly around in the day like this Hummingbird Hawk moth, which hovers like a tiny hummingbird as it sips nectar from flowers.

Hummingbird Hawk Moth

Here are some other moths that you might see flying around during the day.

Mint Moth

Six-spot Burnet Moth

A moth caterpillar usually spins a cocoon of silk, which is a bit like a sleeping bag. A butterfly chrysalis is the hardened body shell of a pupa.

Cinnabar Moth and caterpillar

Pale Tussock Moth cocoon

Garden Tiger Moth and its "woolly bear" caterpillar

There are different families of butterfly, and some butterflies in the same family look very alike. In the UK, there are the nymphalids and browns, the fritillaries, the whites and yellows, the skippers , the coppers and blues, five hairstreaks, one metalmark and one swallowtail, which is the largest butterfly in the UK.

About actual size.

Swallowtail

Wingspan:
80 – 90mm

Host Plant:
milk parsley

About half actual size.

Wingspan:
140 – 190mm

Giant Swallowtail

Even though the Swallowtail is large, it's small compared to the Giant Swallowtail, which can be found across most of the American continent and can be twice as large. Look at the swallow "tails" that make these butterflies easy to identify. There are over 550 species of swallowtail butterfly around the world, most of which are found in tropical climates. In the UK, Swallowtails are mainly seen in the Norfolk Broads.

From the tiniest to the largest butterfly, each one has its own intricate patterns and markings and each species has its own beauty. Males and females can usually be told apart and even butterflies of the same species can look very different, depending on whether their wings are folded or open.

Speckled Wood

Wingspan: 47 – 50mm

Host Plants: False Brome and other grasses

Although caterpillars feed only on their host plant, the adult butterflies drink nectar from many different flowers.

Small Copper

Wingspan: 32 – 35mm

Main Host Plant: Common Sorrel

Butterflies can be quite territorial. Both the Speckled Wood and Small Copper will chase off any males that fly into their territory.

The Speckled Wood is often seen among the treetops feeding on honeydew, a sugary substance made by aphids feeding on tree sap.

Peacocks are one of the UK's best-known and most easily recognisable butterflies.

caterpillar

Peacock

Peacocks may also flash their bright wings and hiss when they feel threatened.

Caterpillars and butterflies have a lot of natural predators, so they have developed various ways to avoid being eaten. Many of them do get eaten, of course, but enough of them manage to trick their enemies and survive. The startling eye markings on this Peacock may make a bird think twice before going after it.

Comma

Wingspan: 55 – 60mm

Main Host Plant: Common Nettle

The Comma butterfly looks a bit like a withered leaf when it has its wings closed, but as soon as it opens them it displays wonderful markings in shades of yellow, orange and brown. Look for the "comma" on the hind wing.

Camouflage is a good way to hide from predators and so butterflies often keep their wings folded. Many of the butterflies that live in grassy areas like meadows blend in by being earth-coloured or looking like a petal or fallen leaf at first glance.

Wingspan: 50 – 55mm

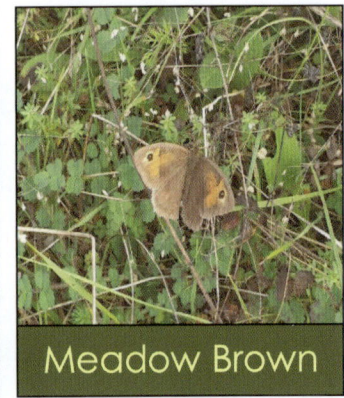

Meadow Brown

Wall

Wingspan: 44 – 46mm

Meadow Brown, Gatekeeper and Wall butterflies all have various grasses as their host plants.

Wingspan: 40 – 47mm

Gatekeeper

Caterpillars have all kinds of tricks for escaping from predators, too. Some make noises, some have bristles or spines, and some can spin a silk thread and jump off a leaf with the thread still attached, so that they can haul themselves back up when the danger has passed. It's rather like rappelling!

When they feel threatened, swallowtail caterpillars try to scare predators away by sticking out "horns" that give off a really bad smell and look a bit like the forked tongue of a snake. The little orange organ on this black swallowtail caterpillar is called an osmeterium.

Spindle Ermine Moth caterpillars

There may be thousands of caterpillars in an Ermine Moth web, but they are harmless.

There are several species of Ermine Moth in the UK and all are white with black spots. Three of the species produce these massive webs from May to June; the trees usually recover.

It looks like over-enthusiastic Halloween decorations, but these photos were taken in June and the webs are spun by the small caterpillars of the Spindle Ermine Moth to protect themselves from predators while they eat.

Part Six – What is it Like to Be a Butterfly?

Imagine floating on the breeze, weighing almost nothing and being swept along by each little gust of wind. You live in a world of colour, feeling and movement.

compound eye

There are 8 species of skipper in the UK. They dart, or "skip" among the flowers.

Small Skipper

Wingspan: 30mm

Host Plants: Yorkshire-fog and other grasses

You are watching the world from eyes made up of thousands of tiny lenses that allow you to look in various directions at the same time. Even though everything is blurry and you can't see things very clearly, those compound eyes also let you see ultraviolet (UV) light, which shows colours and patterns that guide you to the centre of a flower. When you land, your feet and antennae smell and taste the flower and tell you whether you can safely drink the nectar. If they find that you can, your proboscis will unfurl and probe the flower.

UV Light - Violet is at one end of the colour spectrum and UV light is beyond that. Humans can't see UV light, but butterflies and many other insects, birds and even some animals can see it.

Being a butterfly, you are always on the lookout for predators. Your eyesight lets you see everything around you, but when you're on a flower you can also detect vibrations somewhere else on the plant that you might otherwise not have noticed. Even the hairs on your body send signals to your brain, giving you information about your environment that helps you to fly.

Chemoreceptors are the nerve cells on a butterfly that send information to its brain. When a butterfly lands on a leaf, it will drum the leaf with its legs and juices in the plant will send signals to the chemoreceptors that tell the butterfly whether it's on the correct host plant.

Large Skipper

Wingspan: 33 – 35mm

Main Host Plant: Cock's-foot grass

Dingy Skipper

Wingspan: 29mm

Main Host Plant: Bird's-foot-trefoil

A butterfly's antennae are amazing. The tips are similar to the taste buds on the end of our tongues, but they do a lot more than taste. They can help the butterfly in finding flowers or looking for a mate, and they can track the location of the sun to tell a butterfly what time of day it is.

At the base of the antennae, butterflies have a special organ that helps them balance. If one antenna is lost, the butterfly will fly around in circles and be unable to find its way.

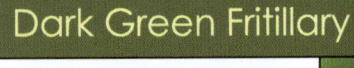

Dark Green Fritillary

Wingspan: 63 - 69mm

Host Plant: Violets

Hairstreaks are small and hard to spot!

White-letter Hairstreak

Wingspan: 36mm

Host Plant: Elms

Green Hairstreak

Various Host Plants

Wingspan: 27 - 34mm

Butterflies don't have noses; they smell through their feet and antennae. Nor do they have mouths like we do, so they can't eat anything solid, they can only drink. Their proboscis is usually coiled, but it can unfurl to reach deep into the heart of a flower. Then it sucks up the nectar like you would drink through a straw. It can also eat pollen by releasing enzymes that turn the pollen into a liquid food. Butterflies are very important to the environment. As they visit flowers for food, they transfer pollen from one plant to another so that the plants can reproduce.

So, next time you see a butterfly, watch it closely. It may seem like a carefree existence, but many butterflies only live for a week or two. Although it looks as though it's floating aimlessly on the breeze, it's actually busy doing butterfly things – looking for nectar and food sources, keeping an eye out for predators, maybe defending its territory, perhaps looking for a mate or a host plant on which to lay eggs, or just looking for water or a place to warm itself in the sun. It may even be on a long journey, flying south in search of warmer weather, or returning to its summer home.

Heath fritillaries at a "puddle party".

Main Host Plants: Common Cow-wheat, Ribwort Plantain, Germander Speedwell

Wingspan: 47 – 50mm

The Heath Fritillary is one of Britain's rarest butterflies, but conservationists are working hard to save it from extinction.

Butterflies get moisture, salt and other nutrients from damp soil. This is called "puddling".

Only about a third of the butterflies found in the UK are likely to be spotted visiting our gardens, even if we grow flowers. Many species live and breed in grassland or woodland and need a habitat that can be hard to create in our gardens. That's why you're more likely to find a Skipper or a Hairstreak in the sunny meadow or woodland clearing of a country park. Understanding a butterfly makes it much easier to find it!

Butterflies have been an important part of many cultures for centuries, symbolising beauty, life and love. There are so many reasons to help butterflies and make sure that children in the future will also be able to go into their garden in summer and watch a butterfly as it sips from a flower or floats away on the breeze. Butterflies really are beautiful!

Silver-studded Blue

Holly Blue

Brown Argus

Brown Hairstreak

Green-veined White

Ringlet

There are some wonderful collective nouns for a group of butterflies. They are known as a rabble, a swarm, a flutter or a kaleidoscope.

Nature Notes

Stinging nettles aren't usually welcome in gardens, but if you have the space they are a fantastic plant for wildlife. They are actually one of the most important plants in the UK for butterflies, as they are the host plants of some of our most widespread species. An area of long grasses and nettles provides a haven for many butterfly species to lay their eggs; cutting back nettles in March and at the end of summer produces fresh growth for caterpillars and stops the nettles from going to seed.

Something more unusual is a climbing plant that can be grown in a pot or over an old fence or wall - humulus lupulus (hops), which is another host plant for the Comma butterfly.

Hops

Large White caterpillar

Cabbages are often grown in vegetable plots and this is what can happen to them. They are the main host plant for both Large and Small White butterflies, but if you grow nasturtiums, another host plant, you can move the caterpillars onto them.

Small White

Wingspan: 48mm

Cabbage Whites are very similar, but (p.11) the Large White is much bigger with more black on the wing's edge.

Nasturtium

A dozen butterfly favourites (bees like them too)!

Butterfly Bush

Sedum

Zinnia

Cosmos

Sunflower

Coneflower

Wallflower

Lavender

Aster

Phlox

Petunia

Hebe

Things We Can Do

Meadow Brown on
wild marjoram,
aka oregano
(origanum vulgare)

1. **Plant flowers.** Native flowers are best; look for plants that grow naturally in your area and are suited to the local climate and conditions. Plants that die back at the end of summer may be hosting overwintering pupae or caterpillars, so leave the garden as natural as possible. It doesn't need clearing; the leaves decay and feed the soil and pruning can be left until spring. Herbs like oregano are great to grow both for pollinators *and* for us to use in the kitchen!

2. **Visit https://butterfly-conservation.org/**
"Butterfly Conservation is a British charity devoted to saving butterflies, moths and their habitats throughout the UK."
Public events are held all year round, including butterfly walks, moth events and conservation days.
Visit www.ukbutterflies.co.uk
This is a wonderful community of butterfly enthusiasts and a great resource for all those wishing to learn more about butterflies.

3. **Become a citizen scientist.** Scientists and conservationists often like to know of sightings, which help them to monitor butterfly populations. Visit **www.gardenbutterflysurvey.org**.

4. **Avoid using pesticides and herbicides.** They are deadly to wildlife and they upset the natural balance of the local ecosystem. Check that the plants you buy have been grown organically and buy native plants if you can find them. There are native nurseries that you can order from online that specifically sell wildflower seeds and plants.

ABOUT THE AUTHOR AND PHOTOGRAPHERS

Annette Meredith is a master gardener, photographer and lifelong student of nature who is passionate about environmental issues and conservation. She was born in England but now lives in North Carolina, where she enjoys encouraging, observing and photographing nature as she works to improve sixty acres of woodland, meadows and organic gardens.

Ian Lindsay is nature photographer who developed an interest in the natural world at an early age. He has been photographing and recording wildlife for over forty-five years and butterflies and moths hold a particular interest for him. He is fascinated by them and says that he never tires of capturing the many stages of their life cycle.

Other books by Annette Meredith:

"Nature on our Doorstep" series for children:

Saving the Bees Helping the Hummingbirds Birds in Our Back Yard
The Secret World of Flowers Butterflies are Beautiful Nature on Our Doorstep
Growing a Green Thumb

Books for Young Children:

Five First Rhyming Readers Nature Rhymes Three First Readers Hello, Mr Tibbs

Nature Books:

A Bluebird Story The Secret World of Trees
Monarchs and Milkweed A Nature Companion

Books for the UK and Europe:

Birds in Our Back Garden Nature on Our Doorstep The Treasure Hunt
Growing Green Fingers All About My Cat French in Pictures

www.natureonourdoorstep.com